THE
LOW CHOLESTEROL
COOKBOOK

Jean Walsh

CHARTWELL
BOOKS INC.

Weights and Measures

All measurements in this book are based on Imperial weights and measures, with American equivalents given in parentheses. Measurements in weight in the Imperial and American system are the same. Measurements in volume are different, and each recipe gives the equivalents. Level spoon measures are used in all the recipes, unless otherwise specified.

Liquid measurements

1 Imperial pint	20 fluid ounces
1 American pint	16 fluid ounces
1 American cup	8 fluid ounces

Metric measures for easy reference

1 oz.	25 g.
8 oz.	225 g.
1 lb.	450 g.
5 fl. oz.	150 ml.
10 fl. oz.	300 ml.
1 Imperial pint	600 ml.
$\frac{1}{4}$ teaspoon	1×1.25 ml. spoon
$\frac{1}{2}$ teaspoon	1×2.5 ml. spoon
1 teaspoon	1×5 ml. spoon
1 tablespoon	1×15 ml. spoon

This edition first published
in the USA 1977 by
Chartwell Books, Inc.
A division of Book Sales, Inc.
110 Enterprise Avenue
Secaucus, New Jersey 07094

© 1977 Octopus Books Limited

ISBN 0 7064 0589 7

Produced and printed in Hong Kong by
Mandarin Publishers Limited
22a Westlands Road, Quarry Bay, Hong Kong

Printed in Hong Kong

CONTENTS

Frontispiece: **NORMANDY CHICKEN** (*Photograph by Fruit Producers' Council*)

Introduction

This is not just another diet cookbook, more a guide to healthy eating. Any diet or restricted eating pattern can become a chore, particularly when it involves cutting out, or cutting down on, favourite foods. This is why so many people let lack of willpower get the better of them, and give up halfway. If the reason for dieting is one of sheer vanity, then it doesn't really matter; but if the main reason is on health grounds, then the diet has to be taken very seriously. Such is the case with a low cholesterol diet. Many people, both men and women, now have to follow a low cholesterol diet on the advice of their doctor. Why? We are now eating much richer food than we used to, in fairly substantial quantities. The richness comes mostly from fats and it has been established by several medical authorities that there is a distinct link between heart complaints, obesity and an excessive consumption of animal fats.

What is cholesterol?

Within animal fat there is a substance called cholesterol, and it can be difficult for the body to burn this up. Cholesterol is not particularly soluble and if we consume too much, it builds up and is stored in the body. The 'plumbing system' of the body can become clogged by these fatty deposits, which leads to mechanical misfunctions of the heart.
This doesn't mean that we should immediately take fright and exclude from our daily diet all foods containing animal fats. A sensible diet should be a balanced and a varied one, and we do in fact need some of the goodness supplied by animal fats.

How to follow a
low cholesterol diet

In order to help our bodies and keep them on a healthy, even keel, all we need to do is moderate our intake of animal fats, and ensure that we get sufficient exercise to burn up the food we eat.
What does this mean? The following simple rules will help to act as a guide:

BEEF RISOTTO MILANAISE *(Photograph: American Rice Council)*

1. Keep meat meals to a minimum, no more than one a day, with as much of the natural fat removed as possible. Meats such as pork, lamb, bacon, liver and kidney should be eaten only occasionally.
2. Use reconstituted low fat skimmed milk powder in place of fresh milk – it is quite palatable, and very easy to get used to.
3. Serve white fish in place of meat in some of your main meals. Oily fish and shellfish are quite high in cholesterol and should be eaten only sparingly.
4. Limit your intake of cheese, eating only very small portions, and use it in sensible quantities when cooking.
5. Don't go mad with eggs, but don't exclude them. If you use them in made-up dishes, such as crêpes and savoury flans, then go steady on the number of the times that you serve 'eggs as eggs', i.e. boiled, poached, scrambled or as omelettes.
6. Use polyunsaturated margarine or vegetable oils for cooking, wherever possible. Unlike butter and other animal-based cooking fats, polyunsaturated margarine is made solely from unsaturated vegetable oils, and contains little or no cholesterol.
7. Grill (broil) rather than fry. With frying you have to introduce extra fat, whereas with grilling (broiling) the natural fat contained in the food is sufficient for cooking, and a good proportion of this fat actually drains off during cooking.
8. Eat a regular amount of natural roughage, such as fresh root vegetables, green vegetables, salads, wholemeal bread and cereals. They help the digestion of other richer foods, and generally help the smooth running of the body.
9. Be wary of many manufactured foods, such as cakes and biscuits (cookies), canned meats, canned milk puddings, pâtés and meat pastes, etc. It is difficult to know exactly how much animal fat is contained in these, so it is better to make your own, and to use fresh ingredients wherever possible.
10. Finally, keep the body in good trim by taking a walk, a swim, or some other form of exercise, each day.

The greatest advantage with a low cholesterol diet is that all the family can join in, including the children, and still enjoy a variety of tasty, appetizing meals. The recipes in this book are for very standard, everyday dishes, many of which are firm favourites already. The only difference is that the ingredients have been carefully balanced to provide a controlled level of cholesterol. The following section shows you how to regulate certain basic ingredients in cooking, without spoiling the appearance, texture and flavour.

Go careful cooking hints

In most of the recipes you will find certain ingredients which are followed by a 'see note' reference to this section. These are 'go careful' ingredients, which are explained as follows.

Note on milk
Most people use a lot of milk, both for drinks and in cooking. Low fat skimmed milk powder has had a lot of the animal fat removed, and makes an excellent substitute for fresh milk. It can be used in any recipe that normally calls for fresh milk. Keep a jug of reconstituted milk powder in the refrigerator, so that you always have it on hand. Reconstitute the milk powder according to the pack instructions – the usual proportions are 2 oz. ($\frac{1}{4}$ cup) milk powder to 1 pint (2$\frac{1}{2}$ cups) water.

Note on cheese
It has already been said that the quantity of cheese eaten should be limited. Serve only small portions of cheese (1 oz. maximum) with biscuits (crackers) or bread. For cooking, use one of the cheeses that has a fairly low fat content, such as Edam or Gouda. If you use harder, full fat cheeses, use them sparingly.

Note on meat
All meat contains fat, even the lean. Generally speaking, the more expensive cuts of meat contain less fat, and it is worth buying very lean meat, even for pies and casseroles. Always trim off as much visible fat as possible. Restrict the number of times you serve pork and lamb, as both are very fatty meats. All sausages (both British and Continental) are high in fat, and should be served only occasionally.

Note on bacon and ham
Like all pork products, bacon and ham are both high in fat. Use them sparingly, selecting the leanest pieces.

Note on liver and kidney
Liver and kidney may appear to be very 'lean' meats, but don't be deceived. They can promote a high level of cholesterol, and it is better to serve them only once a week.

Note on fish and shellfish
White fish (plaice, sole, whiting, cod, etc.) is the lowest in cholesterol content of all fish. Oily fish and shellfish, however, should be eaten only occasionally, in fairly small portions. They do contain valuable nutrients, and should not be excluded completely.

Note on cream

Cream as such, particularly the double (heavy) variety, contains a high percentage of concentrated animal fat, and should be cut out of the daily diet completely. You can use a perfectly acceptable substitute in all recipes calling for cream, as illustrated below.

'Double (Heavy) Cream' For a thick cream to serve with puddings and fruit make up one sachet instant dessert topping with 5 fl. oz. ($\frac{5}{8}$ cup) reconstituted low fat milk. This makes just over $\frac{1}{4}$ pint ($\frac{2}{3}$ cup). For a thick cream to use in the making of hot and cold desserts make up one sachet instant dessert topping with 8 fl. oz. (1 cup) reconstituted low fat milk. This makes approximately $\frac{1}{2}$ pint (1$\frac{1}{4}$ cups).

'Single (Light) Cream' Make up one sachet instant dessert topping with 12 fl. oz. (1$\frac{1}{2}$ cups) reconstituted low fat milk.

Reconstituted instant dessert topping can be used in savoury dishes, but flavourwise, it is better to use low fat natural yoghurt.

'Soured Cream' Make up one sachet instant dessert topping with 12 fl. oz. (1$\frac{1}{2}$ cups) reconstituted low fat milk, and add 1$\frac{1}{2}$ tablespoons vinegar or lemon juice; or use low fat natural yoghurt. This is suitable to use in both sweet and savoury dishes.

This is not a medical book on how to combat heart disease, and it does not give maximum or minimum cholesterol levels. If you suffer from heart trouble, you should consult a doctor as to the quantity of cholesterol you can safely consume per day.

Soups and Appetizers

A soup or appetizer sets the scene for a meal, and colour, texture and flavour all add to the overall appeal. It can be as light or as substantial as you choose, depending on the dishes that are to follow. If the main course is rich and heavy, then it is better to serve something refreshing, and not too filling. The time of year and the weather should also be taken into consideration – on a hot summer's day, hearty soups are out of the question, and a chilled soup or fresh fruit or vegetable appetizer is more the order of the day; save the minestrones and broths for the cold, wet days of autumn and winter.

The flavour of a soup depends very much on the quality of the ingredients that are used. Select fresh, seasonal vegetables, avoiding those that are old and wilted –'sad' vegetables readily spoil the flavour of other ingredients. If you have fish or meat bones available, it is worth making your own stock, otherwise use stock cubes which are quite adequate in flavour. Any left-over gravy gives a good flavour boost to a home-made soup.

Chicken Chowder

2 or 3 rashers (slices) lean bacon
1 onion
$\frac{3}{4}$ pint (2 cups) chicken stock
about 12 oz. ($1\frac{1}{2}$ cups) diced raw
  root vegetables
$\frac{1}{2}$ pint ($1\frac{1}{4}$ cups) milk (see note
  on Milk, page 11)

about 6 oz. (nearly 1 cup) diced
  cooked chicken
3–4 tablespoons sweet corn
seasoning
Garnish:
chopped parsley
paprika

Chop the bacon and the peeled onion. Fry the bacon for a few minutes. Add the onion then cook together until the bacon is crisp. Add the stock. Bring to the boil, put in the vegetables and cook until just tender. Add the milk, chicken, sweet corn and seasoning. Simmer for a few minutes then serve, topped with parsley and paprika.
Serves 4–6.

Variations (see notes on Shellfish, and Bacon and Ham, page 11):

Lobster Chowder: Use the recipe above, but add flaked lobster in place of the chicken. You can make the chowder with chicken stock or simmer the lobster shells to give a fish stock.

Ham Chowder: Use stock from boiling bacon or ham in place of chicken stock. Increase the amount of bacon slightly and reduce the amount of chicken.

Clam Chowder: Use fish stock in place of chicken stock and use about 8 oz. bacon. Add a medium-sized can clams instead of chicken.

Creamed Chicken Soup

Omit the sweet corn and the root vegetables in the Chicken Chowder recipe above. Sieve or emulsify the ingredients, including the cooked chicken. Top with cream (see note on Cream, page 12), before serving.

Salmon Chowder

1 pint (2½ cups) milk (see note
  on Milk, page 11)
medium-sized can sweet corn
medium-sized can salmon

1 oz. (2 tablespoons)
  polyunsaturated margarine
seasoning
chopped parsley

Put the milk and sweet corn into a pan. Bring almost to the
boil. Add the flaked salmon, margarine, seasoning and parsley.
Heat gently for a few minutes.
Serves 4.

Variations:
Use tuna, crabmeat, chopped prawns or flaked white fish in
place of the salmon (see notes on Fish and Shellfish, page 11).
Omit the corn and add raw diced vegetables, such as potatoes,
onions, peas, carrots, to the milk. Simmer steadily for about
15 minutes. Add a little extra milk or white stock, then the
remaining ingredients.

Creamed Kidney Soup

1 onion
4 lambs' kidneys
2 oz. (¼ cup) polyunsaturated
  margarine
½ pint (1¼ cups) stock
1 oz. (¼ cup) flour

¼ pint (⅔ cup) milk
seasoning
¼ pint (⅔ cup) thin cream (see
  notes on Cream, Milk and
  Kidneys, pages 11–12)
2 tablespoons sherry

Chop the onion and kidneys very finely, discarding any
gristle. Heat the margarine and cook the onion and kidneys
for a few minutes. Add the stock. Cover the pan and simmer
for 15 minutes. Blend the flour with the milk and add to the
soup. Season and stir until thickened and smooth. Add the
cream and sherry and heat through without boiling.
Serves 4–5.

SALMON CHOWDER *(Photograph by John West Foods Ltd)*

Crème Chambertin

2 medium-sized onions
2 medium-sized potatoes
2 oz. ($\frac{1}{4}$ cup) polyunsaturated
   margarine
1 pint ($2\frac{1}{2}$ cups) chicken stock
seasoning
1 oz. ($\frac{1}{4}$ cup) flour

$\frac{1}{2}$ pint ($1\frac{1}{4}$ cups) milk
1 large carrot
2 tablespoons chopped fresh herbs,
   or pinch dried herbs
$\frac{1}{2}$ pint ($1\frac{1}{4}$ cups) soured cream
   (see notes on Cream and Milk,
   pages 11–12)

Chop the onions and potatoes. Toss in hot margarine for a few minutes, take care the vegetables do not brown. Add the stock and simmer gently for 30 minutes. Season lightly. Sieve or emulsify the soup and return to the pan. Blend the flour with the milk and stir into the vegetable purée. Continue stirring over a low heat until the mixture thickens. Add the finely grated carrot, herbs, half the soured cream, and a little extra seasoning. Simmer for 5–10 minutes. Do not boil. Top with the remainder of the soured cream.
Serves 6–8.

Variations:
Add small sprigs cooked cauliflower after sieving.
Add thin cream and lemon juice to the soup instead of soured cream.
Creamed Borscht: Grate a medium sized cooked beetroot and add to the soup with the grated carrot, etc.
Chicken Chambertin: Add a little finely diced cooked chicken to the soup with the grated carrot, etc.

Economy hint:
Simmer the carcass of a chicken to produce really first class chicken stock.

To prepare in advance:
Prepare the soup to the stage before adding the carrot, etc. Grate the carrot and keep in a polythene (plastic) bag in the refrigerator. Continue heating as the recipe, but in the top of a double saucepan or basin over hot, but not boiling, water.

Chilled Summer Soup

1 medium-sized lettuce
1 bunch watercress or use a little
  parsley instead
1 medium-sized bunch spring
  onions or scallions
1½ oz. (3 tablespoons)
  polyunsaturated margarine

1½ pints (3¾ cups) chicken stock
  or water and 2 chicken stock
  cubes
1½ oz. (⅜ cup) flour
seasoning
½ pint (1¼ cups) thin cream (see
  note on Cream, page 12)
Garnish:
chopped parsley

Wash and shred the lettuce, discard any tough outer leaves.
Chop the watercress leaves, or enough parsley to give
1 tablespoon. Chop the white part of the onions together with
some of the green stems.
Heat margarine in a saucepan and add the lettuce, watercress
or parsley and spring onions. Lower the heat and cook for 10
minutes, stirring several times so the vegetables do not burn.
Add most of the stock or water and stock cubes. Simmer
gently for 10 minutes, or until the vegetables are tender.
Blend the flour with the remaining stock. Add to the soup and
cook until thickened. Season well. Sieve or emulsify the soup
to give a very smooth purée. If you do this after thickening
the soup a skin will not form.
Allow to become really cold, then whisk in most of the cream.
Serve in a chilled tureen or soup cups. Top with the rest of
the cream and chopped parsley.
Serves 4–6.
Variations:
Use sprigged cauliflower with 1–2 chopped leeks instead of
the lettuce, watercress and onions. Sieve or emulsify as above,
garnish with paprika.
Use about 6 oz. shredded spinach and spring onions or
scallions, but omit the lettuce and watercress. Sieve or
emulsify as above, garnish with cream and parsley.
Use a lettuce, ½ peeled chopped cucumber and 1 chopped
onion together with the grated rind of 2 oranges. Omit the
watercress and spring onions or scallions. Sieve or emulsify
as above. Garnish with diced cucumber, serve with quartered
oranges.

Stuffed Tomatoes

4 large or 6 medium-sized
  tomatoes
salt and pepper
2 oz. (1 cup) fresh white
  breadcrumbs
1 medium-sized onion, grated
1 clove garlic, crushed

2 oz. mushrooms, finely chopped
about 8 blanched almonds,
  finely chopped
1 tablespoon chopped parsley
1 oz. (2 tablespoons)
  polyunsaturated margarine
8–12 olives

Cut the tomatoes in half and scoop out the insides. Season the insides with salt and pepper and turn the tomatoes upside down on a board or plate to drain while preparing the stuffing. Chop the tomato pulp finely and blend with the breadcrumbs, onion, garlic, mushrooms, almonds, parsley and seasoning. Pile back into the tomato cases. Put a small knob of margarine on each tomato and place in an ovenproof dish. Bake, uncovered, in a moderate oven, 350°F., Gas Mark 4 for 15–20 minutes or until golden brown. Garnish each tomato with an olive before serving. **Serves 4-6 as a starter.**

Baked Eggs and Ham

4 oz. sliced cooked lean ham
1 x 10 oz. can mushrooms,
  drained

black pepper
4 eggs
salt

Very lightly grease a baking dish or tin. Put the ham and mushrooms into the dish or tin. Season with pepper. Cover the dish with foil and bake in a moderately hot oven, 400°F., Gas Mark 6, for about 10 minutes..
Remove the dish from the oven and break the eggs over the ham. Season with salt and pepper. Return to the oven and bake for a further 10 minutes or until the whites of the eggs are set.
Serves 2.

STUFFED TOMATOES (*Photograph by Angel Studios*)

Melon Balls with Lemon Sauce

1 melon, see below
2 lemons
little water
2 tablespoons sugar

Garnish:
sprigs of mint
twists of lemon

Buy a ripe Honeydew, Charentais or Cantaloupe melon, or a rather large Ogen melon. Halve the melon, and remove the seeds. Take a vegetable scoop and make balls of the flesh. Chill these. The rather untidy pieces of melon at the bottom of the fruit can be used for the sauce.
Grate enough rind from the lemons to give about 2 teaspoons. Squeeze the juice, measure and add enough water to give $\frac{1}{4}$ pint ($\frac{2}{3}$ cup). Simmer the rind with the liquid and sugar for about 5 minutes. Pour over the odd pieces of melon, then sieve or emulsify in the liquidizer. Taste and add more sugar if wished. This is not really necessary, for the sauce should be both thick and fairly sharp. Spoon into the bottom of 4–6 glasses and top with the melon balls. Garnish with mint and lemon.
Serves 4–6.

Variations:
Sprinkle the balls of melon with a little Crème de Menthe. Freeze canned pineapple juice until lightly frozen; do not allow it to become too hard. Put at the bottom of glasses and top with diced melon or melon balls.

To prepare in advance:
Cut the melon balls and prepare the syrup, but do not blend until 1–2 hours before the meal so the melon does not become over-soft.

New ways to serve:
Toss the melon balls in the syrup and serve as a dessert rather than an hors d'oeuvre. It is delicious with ice cream or with cream (see note on Cream, page 12).

Vegetables and Salads

All vegetables and salad ingredients are allowed on a low cholesterol diet, and they play an important part in balancing other foods.

It is, however, important to choose cooking methods and accompaniments carefully. Fresh vegetables are at their best when served lightly cooked, or even raw for salads, as a lot of their goodness and texture is lost during prolonged cooking. Plain boiled vegetables are more exciting when served with a sauce; choose from the recipes on pages 88 and 90 to make sure that you use permitted ingredients. Don't be tempted to top cooked vegetables with a knob of butter – always use polyunsaturated margarine instead. For frying vegetables, use a pure vegetable oil, or melted polyunsaturated margarine.

With salads you have a completely free choice, as long as you keep a watch on certain 'additional' ingredients, such as cheese and fish. If in doubt, check with the notes on pages 11 and 12. Most salad dressings are based on a vegetable or olive oil, as with the Oil and Vinegar Dressing on page 27.

Spinach Niçoise

1½–2 lb. fresh spinach or about
12 oz. packet frozen spinach
salt
3 oz. (⅜ cup) polyunsaturated
  margarine
2 tablespoons thick cream

pepper
4 large tomatoes
2 onions

4 oz. (1 cup) grated cheese (see
  notes on Cheese and Cream,
  pages 11–12)

Cook the spinach with a little salt, or as on the packet of
frozen spinach. Strain, either sieve or chop finely. Return to
the pan with half the margarine and the thick cream. Heat
gently until a creamy consistency. Add pepper to taste. While
the spinach is cooking, prepare the tomato layer. Skin and
chop the tomatoes and onions. Heat gently in the remaining
margarine until soft. Add the grated cheese, season with
salt and pepper, do not heat again. Put the creamed spinach
into a shallow, very hot, heat-proof dish, top with the hot
tomato and cheese mixture. Heat for a few minutes under the
grill (broiler) and serve at once.
Serves 4–6.

Variation:
A few seedless raisins may be added to the tomato layer
if wished.
Use cooked sprigged cauliflower or cooked sliced courgettes
instead of spinach.

To save time:
Leave frozen spinach in the saucepan at room temperature for
a while so it thaws out; this saves time and adding extra water.

Hawaiian Salad

1 lettuce
1–2 heads chicory (French or
    Belgian endive)
about 8 oz. (1 cup) cottage cheese
fresh or canned pineapple rings

2–3 oranges
1 apple
piece cucumber
oil and vinegar dressing (see
    opposite page)

Prepare the lettuce, put on a flat dish. Wash and separate the chicory leaves, arrange at either end of the dish. Spoon the cottage cheese into the centre of the lettuce, garnish with halved pineapple rings, orange segments and apple and cucumber slices (both dipped in oil and vinegar).
Serves 4.

Note: About 2 tablespoons mayonnaise can be blended into the cheese if wished.

Variations:
Use peach slices instead of pineapple.
Use cooked well drained prunes instead of the orange segments.
Top the cottage cheese with halved walnuts or other nuts.

Salad Marguerite

3–4 eggs
small cauliflower
8 oz. French (green) or haricots
    verts beans
seasoning

8 oz. potatoes
small bunch asparagus or medium-
    sized can asparagus
mayonnaise
lettuce

Hard boil the eggs. Divide the cauliflower into neat sprigs and cut the ends from the beans. Halve these if fairly long. Cook the cauliflower and beans in salted water. The potatoes may be cooked in their jackets, or peeled or scraped and should be boiled steadily in salted water. Cook the asparagus in salted water or drain canned asparagus. Shell the eggs and allow to cool. Drain the cooked vegetables; skin the potatoes if these were cooked in the skins. Cut the potatoes and asparagus into neat pieces.

Mix the vegetables with mayonnaise and season generously. Allow to cool. Shred the lettuce, put into a bowl. Pile the mixed vegetables on top of this and coat with a little more mayonnaise. Cut the eggs into segments. Take out the yolks and chop these finely. Arrange the egg whites over the top of the salad to look like flower petals and place the yolks in the centre to resemble the stamens of the flowers.

Serves 4–6.

Variations:
Omit the beans and add diced tongue or cooked ham.
Use another mixture of vegetables in season, but if no meat is used the beans add to the protein content of this dish.
Blue cheese salad: Make the salad as above, but omit the eggs. Crumble about 6 oz. Danish Blue cheese (see note on Cheese, page 11). Blend well with the mayonnaise, and then mix with the vegetables.

Oil and Vinegar Dressing

3 tablespoons olive or good salad oil
up to 1 teaspoon French mustard
good shake salt

pinch sugar or little more if wished
shake pepper
$1\frac{1}{2}$ tablespoons lemon juice or vinegar

Blend the oil into the mustard, then add the other ingredients. If wished put into the liquidizer goblet and mix together.
It is worthwhile making a larger quantity and storing it in a screw-topped jar. Shake well before using.

Potatoes Dauphine

8 oz. (1 cup) mashed potatoes or use instant potatoes and prepare as instructions on the packet
seasoning
Choux pastry:
2 oz. ($\frac{1}{4}$ cup) polyunsaturated margarine

$\frac{1}{4}$ pint ($\frac{2}{3}$ cup) water
3 oz. ($\frac{3}{4}$ cup) flour
2 eggs plus 1 egg yolk
seasoning
oil for deep frying

Beat the mashed potatoes with seasoning until very smooth or make up the instant potatoes.
Put the margarine and water into a pan and heat until the fat has melted. Remove the pan from the heat, add the flour and stir over a low heat until the flour mixture forms a dry ball. Gradually beat the eggs and egg yolk into the choux pastry then blend in the potato purée. Taste, add more seasoning if required.
Heat the oil. To test temperature, drop in a cube of day-old bread. If the temperature is correct it will turn golden brown in just over 30 seconds. Either pipe or spoon small balls of the mixture into the hot oil and deep fry for a few minutes until golden brown. Drain on absorbent paper, serve at once.
Serves 4–6.

Variations:
The above recipe gives a particularly light version. You can use up to 1 lb. (2 cups) mashed potatoes to the amount of choux pastry given.
Add 2–3 tablespoons finely grated cheese (see note on Cheese, page 11) to the mixture, with or after adding the potatoes. Flavour with chopped parsley and/or nutmeg.

To prepare in advance:
These cannot be kept hot for a very long period since they lose their light crispness. It is better to prepare the potatoes, then prepare the choux pastry, put the mixture together and cook just before required.

POTATOES DAUPHINE
(Photograph by Cadbury Schweppes Food Advisory Service, Bournville, Birmingham)

French Fried Fennel

1 fennel root	seasoning
2 oz. ($\frac{1}{2}$ cup) flour	oil for frying
1 egg	
6 tablespoons ($\frac{1}{2}$ cup) milk	
(see note on Milk, page 11)	

Wash the fennel and slice the white root. Save the green
leaves for garnish. Separate into rings. Mix the flour, egg and
milk into a smooth batter. Season well. Dip the rings of fennel
into the batter. Heat a pan of oil for deep frying. Drop the
coated rings of fennel into the hot oil and deep fry for 2–3
minutes. This gives a cooked, crisp outside, without losing the
natural firmness of the vegetable.
Serves 4.

Cheese, Bacon and Potato Salad

Dice cheese neatly (see note on Cheese, page 11). Fry several
chopped bacon rashers (slices) (see notes on Bacon and Ham,
page 11), and mix with diced, cooked potatoes and the
cheese, while the bacon is still hot. When cool, blend with a
little mayonnaise plus a dash of vinegar or lemon juice, to
counteract the richness of the bacon. Serve on a bed of lettuce
or watercress, and garnish with sliced raw mushrooms, sliced
tomatoes and cucumber.

Chef's Salad

This is a splendid way of using any small amounts of various
meats (see note on Meat, page 11). Take any meats available –
a good combination is ham, tongue, chicken and beef – and
cut into thin strips. Cut cheese into similar size strips (see note
on Cheese, page 11). Mix meat and cheese lightly with a little
mayonnaise, or a little oil and vinegar, and season well. Make
a bed of mixed salad in a bowl, top with the meat and cheese
mixture, and garnish with chopped nuts.

Fish

Fish can be divided into six main categories, for ease of identification: white fish (plaice, haddock, cod, etc.), oily fish (herring, mackerel, whitebait, etc.), freshwater fish (carp, salmon, trout, etc.), smoked fish (smoked haddock, kipper, smoked salmon, etc.), shellfish (crab, lobster, mussels, etc.), and preserved fish, which covers canned and frozen fish.

White fish is the only 'safe' fish for people on a low cholesterol diet, and even some of these fish are quite rich in fat, such as halibut. It is advisable to keep to plaice, sole and haddock, if you serve fish meals regularly. The other fish, such as smoked fish and shellfish, should be served only occasionally, in fairly small portions, as they have a high content of fish oil. The best way of serving these richer fish is in a made-up dish, where they are used in small quantities and extended with other ingredients. Suggested sauces, suitable for serving with grilled (broiled), fried or poached fish, can be found on pages 88 and 90.

Fish in a Jacket

1 lb. frozen puff pastry or rough
   puff pastry made with 8 oz.
   (2 cups) flour, etc. (see page 62)
4 very large or 6 smaller fillets
   white fish
seasoning
Sauce:
1 oz. (2 tablespoons)
   polyunsaturated margarine

1 oz. ($\frac{1}{4}$ cup) flour
$\frac{1}{4}$ pint ($\frac{2}{3}$ cup) milk (see note on
   Milk, page 11)
about 4 oz. mushrooms
Glaze:
1 egg
1 tablespoon water
Garnish:
sliced lemon and parsley

Prepare the pastry and roll out thinly, then cut into 4 or 6
squares, large enough to cover the fish. Lay the fillets flat on a
board, season lightly.

Make a sauce with the margarine, flour and milk. Add the
chopped uncooked mushrooms and season well. Spread over
half of each fillet. Fold the other half of the fish over the
sauce. Lay on the squares of pastry, moisten the edges, fold
over in triangles and seal the edges. Lift on to a baking sheet,
brush with a little beaten egg, blended with water.

Bake for 10 minutes just above the centre of a very hot oven,
475°F, Gas Mark 8, then lower the heat to moderate,
350–375°F, Gas Mark 4–5 and cook for a further 20–25
minutes until golden brown and well risen. Garnish with
lemon and parsley and serve hot.

Serves 4–6.

Variation:
If preferred, blend flaked cooked fish with a thick sauce and
chopped mushrooms and use as a filling for the pastry.

To complete the meal:
Serve a green salad and fresh fruit.

To serve for a buffet:
Make the pastry into 8–10 smaller squares; fill as the variation
above. Bake for a slightly shorter period.

Rolled Fillets of Fish

8 medium fillets of skinned white   coating (a) or (b), see below
   fish   cooking oil, see below

Roll the fillets and secure with wooden cocktail sticks. Dip in
the selected coating (a) or (b); remove the sticks before frying.
(a) **Egg and breadcrumb coating**: Coat fish with seasoned
flour and then with beaten egg and fine crisp breadcrumbs.
You can use fine soft crumbs if preferred. It is a good idea to
coat the fish with a very thin layer of flour before the egg, as
this helps the final coating to adhere to the fish. 1 egg plus
about 2 oz. ($\frac{1}{2}$ cup) crisp breadcrumbs should coat 4 portions
(8 small to medium fillets).
(b) **Batter coating**: The following quantities are enough to
coat 4 portions (8 small to medium fillets). Sieve 4 oz. (1 cup)
flour, plain (all-purpose) or self-raising, with a pinch salt.
Add 1 egg and about 12 tablespoons milk (see note on Milk,
page 11). When coating in batter, dip the fish in seasoned
flour first. Dip in the batter; allow any surplus batter to drop
back into the basin.
Serves 4 as a main dish.

Cooking oil for frying:
Make sure the pan of cooking oil is not over-filled, as the
level will rise when the fish is placed in the pan. Test the
temperature of the oil – it should be 365°F. Place the empty
frying basket in the hot cooking oil so it becomes coated, as
this prevents the fish sticking to the mesh. Lift the warmed
basket from the oil, and lower the coated fish into the basket.

Timing:
Thick or rolled fillets take about 4 minutes. **Thin fillets** take
about 3 minutes. Thick steaks or whole **fish take about 5–6**
minutes.
Lift the fish from the pan and allow the **basket** to remain over
the top of the pan for a few seconds for **any surplus fat to drop**
back into the pan. Drain on absorbent paper and serve. Deep
fried fish can be served with tartare sauce.

Seafood Pie

1½ lb. white fish, inexpensive
  kind
about ½ pint (1¼ cups) fish stock
  or water
seasoning
Sauce:
2 oz. (¼ cup) polyunsaturated
  margarine

2 oz. (½ cup) flour
1 pint (2½ cups) milk, or milk and
  fish stock (see note on Milk,
  page 11)
few prawns (shrimp)
about 1 lb. mashed potato
little polyunsaturated margarine

Poach the fish, either in the fish stock or in the water and
seasoning. Drain and flake the fish; use the liquid as part of
the sauce if wished. Make the sauce as the recipe on page 88.
Mix the sauce and fish, add the prawns (shrimp). Put into a
pie dish and top with the mashed potato and a little margarine.
Bake for approximately 30 minutes just above the centre of a
moderately hot oven, 375°F, Mark 5.
Serves 4–5.

Fish Pie Americaine

2–3 rashers (slices) streaky bacon
1–2 onions
3 tomatoes
1 oz. (¼ cup) flour

¾ pint (2 cups) chicken or fish
  stock
1–1½ lb. white fish
seasoning
1 lb. (2 cups) mashed potato

Chop the bacon, onions and skinned tomatoes. Fry the bacon
2–3 minutes to extract the fat. Add the onions and then the
tomatoes and cook for several minutes. Stir in the flour, then
gradually blend in the stock. Bring to the boil and cook until
thickened. Cook the fish – either by baking or poaching in
well seasoned water. Flake and add to the sauce; season well.
Put into a pie dish, top with mashed potato and bake for
approximately 30 minutes just above the centre of a
moderately hot to hot oven, 375–400°F, Mark 5–6.
Serves 5–6.

Plaice (Flounder) in Cream

1 lb. (2 cups) cooked mashed
  potatoes
seasoning
2 oz. ($\frac{1}{4}$ cup) polyunsaturated
  margarine
4 large or 8 small plaice
  (flounder) fillets

3 oz. ($\frac{3}{4}$ cup) mushrooms
3–4 rashers (slices) lean bacon
$\frac{1}{4}$ pint ($\frac{2}{3}$ cup) thick cream (see
  notes on Cream and Bacon,
  pages 11–12)
Garnish:
tomato
parsley

Beat the potatoes with seasoning and 1 oz. (2 tablespoons)
margarine. Put into a cloth bag with a $\frac{1}{2}$-inch large star nozzle;
and pipe a border round the edge of a shallow oven-proof
dish. Skin the fillets of fish, or ask the fishmonger to do this.
If using frozen fish allow to defrost. Slice the mushrooms and
chop the bacon. Heat the remaining margarine and fry the
mushrooms and bacon in this for a few minutes. Spoon into
the centre of the fish fillets. Roll up the fillets from the tail to
the head, securing with wooden cocktail sticks and put into
the dish. Season the cream. Pour over the fish. Cover the dish
lightly with foil, do not press this down and spoil the potato
piping. Bake in the centre of a moderate oven, 350–375°F,
Mark 4–5, for 15 minutes until the fish is tender; do not
over-cook.
Meanwhile halve the tomato or cut in a Van-Dyke design, and
bake for a few minutes in the oven. Remove the foil and
cocktail sticks from the fillets, and garnish with the tomato
and parsley. Serve at once.
Serves 4.

Variations:
Omit the cream in the recipe above and use a white sauce
made with 1 oz. (2 tablespoons) polyunsaturated margarine,
1 oz. ($\frac{1}{4}$ cup) flour and $\frac{1}{2}$ pint ($1\frac{1}{4}$ cups) milk, or milk and fish
stock (see note on Milk, page 11).
As a change make the sauce with $\frac{1}{2}$ pint ($1\frac{1}{4}$ cups) tomato
juice instead of milk.
Omit the mushroom and bacon stuffing and use a packet of
parsley and thyme mixture, or a little flaked canned tuna fish
or salmon.

Meat and Poultry

'One man's meat is another man's poison' is a true statement when applied to anyone on a low cholesterol diet. *All* meat contains fat, and it is necessary to keep a careful watch on the type and quantity you eat. As a general guide, all meats that look fatty contain quite a lot of fat (lamb, pork, etc.). But don't be deceived by the ham and kidneys of this world – they too are quite high in fat content.

If you eat meat in moderation, using the leanest cuts possible, you won't go far wrong. They may prove to be a little more expensive but, where health is concerned, it's worth it.

The method of cooking that you choose doesn't really matter, as long as animal fat isn't used. Polyunsaturated margarine can be used for roasting and shallow frying, and vegetable oil for shallow and deep frying.

There are many dishes that make a little meat go a long way, and you will find several such recipes in this section, e.g. Beef Risotto Milanaise (page 39), Lamb and Raisin Patties (page 43), Sweet Curry (page 48), and Chicken Supreme (page 56).

Beef Risotto Milanaise

2 tablespoons oil
2 onions
1–2 cloves garlic
1 lb. minced (ground) beef
1 medium-sized can tomatoes
4 carrots

seasoning
1 bay leaf
8 oz. (1 cup) long grain rice
1 pint (2½ cups) water
1 tablespoon tomato purée
Garnish:
parsley

Heat the oil in a pan. Peel and cut the onions into thin rings and slice the garlic. Toss the onions and garlic in the oil until the onions are transparent. Put a few rings on one side for garnish. Add the beef to the pan, stir well to break up any lumps. Add the tomatoes and the liquid from the can, the roughly chopped carrots, the tomato purée, seasoning and bay leaf. Cook gently in a covered pan for 45 minutes, stirring once or twice.

Put the rice and the cold water into a saucepan with $\frac{1}{2}$–1 teaspoon salt. Bring the water to the boil, stir briskly then cover the pan. Lower the heat and cook for approximately 15 minutes until the rice is tender and the liquid absorbed. Fork the rice on to a hot dish. Spoon the beef mixture in the centre and garnish with onion rings and a sprig of parsley.
Serves 4–5.

Variations:
Omit a little of the juice from the canned tomatoes and use red wine instead or if you like to use all the liquid from the can plus red wine, blend 1 tablespoon flour into the onion, garlic and meat mixture before blending in the tomatoes, etc.
Country Hotpot: Prepare the meat mixture as the basic recipe, but only cook for 25 minutes, then put into a deep casserole. Cover with thinly sliced raw potatoes and a little seasoning and polyunsaturated margarine. Bake for 45 minutes to 1 hour in the centre of a moderate oven, 350°F, Gas Mark 4. Top with chopped parsley.
Serves 4–5.

Steak and Kidney Pie

Filling:
1¼–1½ lb. stewing steak (see note
   on Meat, page 11)
about 8 oz. ox-kidney
nearly 1 oz. (¼ cup) flour
seasoning
2 oz. (¼ cup) polyunsaturated
   margarine
¾ pint (2 cups) stock

flaky pastry made with 6 oz.
   (1½ cups) flour, etc. (see page
   62)
Glaze:
1 egg plus 1 tablespoon water or
   a little milk (see note on Milk,
   page 11)

Cut the steak and kidney into neat pieces. Blend the flour
and seasoning. Roll the meat in the seasoned flour and fry
gently in the hot margarine. Blend the stock gradually into the
meat. Bring to the boil and cook until thickened. Cover the
pan very tightly and simmer gently until the meat is tender
(2–2¼ hours). Make sure the liquid does not evaporate too
much and add more if necessary.
Make the flaky pastry (page 62) while the meat is cooking.
Spoon the meat and a little gravy into a 2–3 pint (5–7½ cup)
pie dish, allow to cool; cover with the pastry. Flake the pastry
edges with a knife to encourage it to rise. Make a slit in the
pastry so that the steam escapes during baking and arrange
pastry leaves, made from the trimmings, on top. Beat the egg
with the water. Brush over the pastry to glaze or use milk.
Stand the pie dish on a baking tray, as a precaution in case
any liquid boils out. Bake in the centre of a hot to very hot
oven, 450–475°F, Mark 7–8 for 15–20 minutes. Reduce heat
to 350–375°F, Mark 4–5 and cook for a further 30–35
minutes, until the pastry is cooked and golden brown.
Serves 6.

Variations:
Add sliced onions or other vegetables to the steak and kidney.
Use a little red wine in the gravy in place of all stock.
Plate pie: Prepare the steak mixture but use only 1¼ lb. meat
and just under ½ pint (1¼ cups) stock to give a drier mixture.
Double the amount of pastry. Use half to line a 9-inch shallow
dish, put in the cooled meat mixture. Cover with the pastry
and bake as the main recipe.

40

Ragoût of Beef and Prunes

1 pint (2½ cups) brown stock
about 18 prunes
1¼ lb. chuck steak (see note on
  Meat, page 11)
seasoning
1 oz. (¼ cup) flour

2 oz. (¼ cup) polyunsaturated
  margarine
1 tablespoon tomato purée
2 bay leaves
4–5 tomatoes

Heat the stock, pour over the prunes and soak for about 12 hours, unless using tenderized prunes which need soaking for 1 hour only. Dice the meat, roll in the seasoned flour and cook in the hot margarine for a few minutes to seal the meat. Strain the stock from the prunes, and add to the meat. Bring to the boil and cook until thickened. Add the tomato purée, about 6 finely chopped prunes and the bay leaves. Cover the pan and simmer for 1¾ hours. Add the rest of the prunes and cook for a further 15 minutes. Skin the tomatoes if wished, add to the ragout and cook for 15 minutes.
Serves 4–5.

Variations:
The above recipe is both an economical and pleasant one and it can be altered in so many different ways.
Omit the prunes and use a few raisins instead; add these half way through the cooking so they do not become too soft.
Use dried apricots instead of dried prunes, soaking these in the same way as the prunes. When using apricots omit the tomato purée and flavour with the grated rind and juice of 1 lemon plus 2 teaspoons sugar.
Use ale instead of stock in the basic recipe.
Use chicken joints instead of beef and reduce the cooking time to 45 minutes instead of the 1¾ hours, then add the rest of the prunes and continue as the basic recipe. When cooking chicken use chicken stock or chicken stock mixed with white wine instead of brown stock.

Lamb and Raisin Patties

1 lb. uncooked lean lamb
(preferably cut from the leg)
1 oz. (2 tablespoons)
polyunsaturated margarine
1 oz. ($\frac{1}{4}$ cup) flour
$\frac{1}{4}$ pint ($\frac{2}{3}$ cup) brown stock
3 oz. ($\frac{1}{2}$ cup) raisins

1 tablespoon chopped parsley
seasoning
Coating:
1 egg
2–3 oz. crisp breadcrumbs
oil for frying

Mince (grind) the lamb. Heat the margarine, then stir in the flour and cook for 2 or 3 minutes. Gradually blend in the stock. Bring to the boil, add the raisins, then stir until thickened (by adding the raisins at this stage you make them more moist). Stir in the parsley and lamb, then season well. Allow the mixture to cool. As this is rather soft form into 8 small cakes and chill well before coating. Coat in beaten egg and breadcrumbs, then fry in hot oil until crisp and golden brown on both sides. Lower the heat and fry steadily for another 5–6 minutes to make sure the lamb is thoroughly cooked.
Serves 4.

Variations:
To make a firmer textured patty add 2 oz. (1 cup) soft breadcrumbs to the mixture.
Omit the raisins and add chopped chutney instead (this is very moist so be a little sparing with the stock or use the version including breadcrumbs).

To use cooked meat:
Use minced (ground) cooked lamb. You can use the basic recipe or the variation above that includes breadcrumbs.
Savoury lamb patties:
Increase the amount of margarine to 2 oz. ($\frac{1}{4}$ cup) and fry a chopped onion and 1–2 crushed garlic cloves before proceeding with the recipe.

Kidney Kebabs with Orange Sauce

Sauce:
2 oranges
$\frac{1}{2}$ pint (1$\frac{1}{4}$ cups) brown stock
1 oz. ($\frac{1}{4}$ cup) cornflour
   (cornstarch)
1 oz. (2 tablespoons)
   polyunsaturated margarine
seasoning
$\frac{1}{2}$–1 teaspoon sugar
To serve:
boiled rice

Kebabs:
8–12 skinned whole or halved
lambs' kidneys (see note on
Kidneys, page 11)
seasoning
pinch mixed dried herbs
about 12 mushrooms
12 small cocktail onions

4 rashers (slices) bacon
2 oz. ($\frac{1}{4}$ cup) melted
   polyunsaturated margarine

Pare the rind very thinly from the oranges and simmer this
in half the stock for about 5 minutes. Strain, return to the pan.
Blend cornflour (cornstarch) with rest of the stock, add to the
liquid in the pan with the juice of the oranges, the
margarine, seasoning and sugar. Bring to the boil, cook gently
and stir until smooth and thickened.
Meanwhile, roll the kidneys in seasoning and herbs, put on to
4 metal skewers with the mushrooms, onions and halved
bacon rashers (slices) in neat rolls. Brush with melted
margarine and cook under a hot grill (broiler) for 8 minutes.
Turn several times during cooking, so the food cooks evenly.
Serve on a bed of boiled rice with the orange sauce.
Serves 4.

Note: extra orange segments can be added to the sauce, if
liked.

Variations:
The kidneys may be placed on well greased foil on the pan
and cooked with the other ingredients under the grill (broiler).
Kidneys in Port wine sauce: Cook the kidneys as above or
fry or grill (broil). Omit the oranges and add 4 tablespoons
port wine instead.

Meat Loaf

1 tablespoon polyunsaturated
  margarine
2 oz. ($\frac{1}{2}$ cup) dried
  breadcrumbs
2 lb. lean minced (ground)
  beef (see note on Meat, page
  11)
1 medium-sized onion, finely
  chopped

1 teaspoon seasoned salt*
$\frac{1}{2}$ teaspoon seasoned pepper*
dash garlic salt
$\frac{1}{4}$ teaspoon mixed dried herbs
2 tablespoons
  concentrated tomato purée
1 egg

*If you do not have any seasoned salt and pepper, use ordinary salt and pepper
and add $\frac{1}{2}$ stock cube dissolved in 1 tablespoon (1$\frac{1}{4}$ T) boiling water to the beef.*

Grease a 2-lb. loaf tin with the margarine, then coat with some of
the breadcrumbs. Put the remaining ingredients into a mixing
bowl and mix well, using first a large fork and then a spoon. Pack
the mixture into the loaf tin. Bake in a moderately hot oven,
375°F., Gas Mark 5 for 1$\frac{1}{4}$ hours. Serve either hot or cold. If
serving hot, allow to stand for 10 minutes before slicing.
Serves 6–8.

Cidered Liver

1 lb. lamb's or pig's liver
  (see note on Liver, page 11)
1 oz. ($\frac{1}{4}$ cup) flour
seasoning
3 oz. ($\frac{3}{8}$ cup) polyunsaturated
  margarine
2 dessert apples

1 large onion
$\frac{1}{2}$ pint (1$\frac{1}{4}$ cups) dry cider
To serve:
cooked rice or creamed potato
Garnish:
black and green olives

Cut the liver into fingers, coat with the flour and seasoning.
Heat half the margarine in the pan and fry the liver for a few
minutes only, put on one side. Heat the rest of the margarine
and fry rings of apple (cored but not peeled) and thinly sliced
onion until golden coloured. Add the cider and simmer until
the apple and onion are tender. Replace the liver and heat
through. Serve in a border of cooked rice or creamed potato

(dehydrated potato is very quick and ideal for this purpose). Garnish with a few black and green olives.
Serves 4.

Variations:

Creamed liver: Use the method of cooking above, but omit the apples. Use only ¼ pint (⅔ cup) cider or white wine and blend in ¼ pint (⅔ cup) thin cream (see note on Cream, page 12), just before serving.

Paprika liver: Use sliced tomatoes instead of apples. Blend 1–2 teaspoons paprika with the flour and seasoning. Use either cider as the basic recipe or white wine or stock. Serve with cooked noodles.

Normandy Chicken

1 small roasting chicken
1 oz. (2 tablespoons) polyunsaturated margarine
1 tablespoon oil
1 onion, chopped
1 garlic clove, crushed
3 rashers (slices) streaky bacon, de-rinded and chopped

1 oz. (¼ cup) flour
¾ pint (2 cups) dry cider
2 eating apples
¼ pint (⅔ cup) single (light) cream (see note on Cream, page 12)
1 tablespoon chopped parsley

Cut the chicken into 4 joints. Heat margarine and oil in a large saucepan and fry the chicken on both sides until golden brown. Remove from the pan and put on a plate. You will probably find it easiest to cook 2 joints only at a time. Add the onion, garlic and bacon to the fat in the pan and cook for about 5 minutes, or until the onion is golden. Stir in the flour and cook for 1 minute. Gradually stir in the cider and bring to the boil. Return the chicken to the pan, cover and simmer gently for 30 minutes. Core and dice the apples and stir into the chicken with the cream. Heat for 1–2 minutes without boiling, then turn into a heated serving dish and sprinkle with chopped parsley.
Serves 4.

Sweet Curry

2 medium-sized onions
1–2 cloves garlic
2 oz. ($\frac{1}{4}$ cup) polyunsaturated
   margarine
1 small sweet apple
1–2 grated carrots
1 medium-sized can pineapple,
   guavas or mangoes
$\frac{1}{2}$–1 tablespoon curry powder
$\frac{1}{2}$–1 tablespoon curry paste
1 tablespoon flour
$\frac{1}{2}$ pint (1$\frac{1}{4}$ cups) brown stock
1–2 tablespoons desiccated
   coconut, or grated fresh coconut
1–2 tablespoons sultanas (golden
   raisins)
1–2 tablespoons chutney

1–1$\frac{1}{4}$ lb. uncooked beef (see note
   on Meat, page 11)
1 teaspoon sugar
1 teaspoon lemon juice or vinegar
seasoning
Accompaniments:
6–8 oz. ($\frac{3}{4}$–1 cup) long grain rice
saffron powder, optional
chutney
sliced peppers and tomatoes
Poppadums
Bombay duck
nuts
raisins
grated coconut
sliced banana
rings of raw onion or spring onions

Chop the peeled onions and crush the cloves of garlic. Toss in
the hot fat. Peel and slice the apple, add to the onion mixture
with the carrots and most of the other fruit and the curry
powder and paste, and flour. Fry gently for several minutes,
stirring well to prevent the mixture burning. Gradually blend
in the stock and $\frac{1}{4}$ pint ($\frac{2}{3}$ cup) syrup from the can of fruit,
and bring to the boil; cook until slightly thickened. Put the
coconut, sultanas (raisins) and chutney into the sauce, then
add the diced meat.
For special occasions choose diced topside (top round), rump
or fresh brisket; for economy, choose diced chuck or flank
steak. Simmer for about 1 hour in a tightly covered pan then
add the sugar, lemon juice or vinegar and seasoning. Taste the
sauce and add more sweetening or seasoning as desired. Cover
the pan again and continue cooking for a further 1$\frac{1}{2}$–2 hours.
To cook the rice put this with about 2$\frac{1}{2}$ times the amount of
cold water, i.e. to 8 oz. (1 cup) rice use 1 pint (2$\frac{1}{2}$ cups) cold
water in a saucepan with a lid. Add salt and pepper and a

pinch saffron powder if desired. Bring to the boil, stir
briskly, cover the pan tightly and allow to simmer for
approximately 15 minutes or until the rice has absorbed the
water and is tender.

Arrange the curry in a border of saffron or plain rice or serve
the rice in a separate dish. Garnish the curry with the
remaining pieces of fruit just before serving. Arrange all the
accompaniments in dishes so everyone may help themselves.
The Poppadums should be fried in a very little fat until crisp.
The Bombay duck, which is a dried fish, should be sprinkled
over each portion of curry.

Serves 4–6.

Variations:

The curry sauce, see the basic recipe, is a good basic one.
You can adjust this by omitting the pineapple or other fruit;
by substituting water or white stock for the brown stock and
by increasing or decreasing the amounts of curry powder and
curry paste.

Make this sauce and use it to curry fish, chicken, etc.

To prepare in advance:

A curry sauce is far better if it is prepared and cooked the
day before being required. It can be prepared, cooked and
frozen very successfully too.

The uncooked meat or fish may be put into the sauce, then
cooked on the following day. In this way it becomes
impregnated with the curry flavour.

The rice may be cooked lightly, rinsed in cold water, then
spread on to flat oven-proof dishes, covered with greased
greaseproof paper and warmed in the coolest part of the oven,
or it can be warmed in a covered basin over boiling water.

If you cook the curry in a covered casserole, after making the
sauce, etc., it needs no attention.

Curried Meat Balls

1½ lb. beef, or choose a mixture
   of beef and veal (see note on
   Meat, page 11)
2 medium-sized onions
1 oz. (2 tablespoons)
   polyunsaturated margarine
½ teaspoon ground ginger
1–2 teaspoons curry powder
2 oz. (1 cup) soft breadcrumbs
2 egg yolks
3–4 tablespoons thick cream
For frying and the sauce:
3 oz. (⅜ cup) polyunsaturated
   margarine

1 oz. (¼ cup) flour
1–2 teaspoons curry powder
½ pint (1¼ cups) white stock
¼ pint (⅔ cup) thin cream or milk
   (see notes on Milk and Cream,
   pages 11–12)
seasoning
Garnish:
1–2 green peppers
3–4 tomatoes
cooked rice

Mince (grind) the meat very finely. Chop the onions finely or grate coarsely. Heat margarine in a pan, stir in the onions and cook gently until nearly soft. Add the ginger and curry powder then the meat. Blend very thoroughly, then stir in the crumbs and egg yolks and mix well. Gradually add enough cream to give a soft creamy texture. Put into a cool place for about 30 minutes to stiffen slightly. Make into small balls the size of little walnuts. Heat the margarine in a large frying pan. Put in the meat balls and brown, turning several times. Lift the meat balls out of the pan on to a large plate.

Blend the flour with the fat remaining in the pan and cook for 1–2 minutes. Add the curry powder, then blend in the stock and bring to the boil. Cook gently until thickened, stir in the cream or milk and seasoning. Replace the meat balls and simmer gently for about 10 minutes.

Spoon the balls and sauce on to a very hot dish, garnish with rings of pepper, slices of tomato and the hot rice.
Serves 5–6.

Variation:
Creamed veal curry: Follow the recipe above, but fry small pieces of veal fillet in the margarine instead of meat balls.

Chicken Espagnole

8 joints young chicken
1 oz. ($\frac{1}{4}$ cup) flour
seasoning
2 oz. ($\frac{1}{4}$ cup) polyunsaturated
   margarine
1 tablespoon olive oil
2 large onions or about 8 small
   onions
1–2 cloves garlic

1 lb. tomatoes
$\frac{1}{2}$ pint (1$\frac{1}{4}$ cups) chicken stock, or
   water and a chicken stock cube
4 oz. (1 cup) small mushrooms
Garnish:
chopped parsley

Wash and dry the chicken, roll in flour, blended with a generous amount of seasoning. Heat margarine and oil in a pan, toss the chicken in this until golden brown. Put it on a plate, and then toss the thinly sliced or whole onions in the remaining margarine and oil for 5 minutes. If you like a strong garlic flavour, crush the cloves of garlic and fry with the onions; if you do not like this flavour to be too strong, add the whole cloves of garlic with the onions but remove after 2–3 minutes.

Skin the tomatoes, chop, if very large, and add to the onions, together with the stock, or water and stock cube. Bring to the boil. Add the mushrooms and season well. Put the chicken joints into the pan, but keep them above the level of the liquid if possible. If you like plenty of sauce cover the pan, so the liquid does not evaporate. If you prefer dishes less moist, then leave the lid off the pan for the last 15 minutes. Cook over a low heat for 30–35 minutes. Serve topped with chopped parsley. If preferred, transfer the mixture to a casserole to cook. Cover and allow about 45 minutes to 1 hour in a very moderate to moderate oven, 325–350°F, Mark 3–4. **Serves 4 generous portions.**

Variation:
Add 1–2 sliced green or red peppers to the ingredients above. If you wish the peppers to remain fairly firm in texture add them to the pan or casserole about 10 minutes before the chicken is cooked.

Serving Roast Poultry

Carving:
You may prefer to carve or joint the birds and serve each
person at the table. Use a sharp knife or knives for carving,
and poultry scissors if preferred for jointing chickens or duck.
The easiest way to carve larger chickens, turkey and goose is
to ease the leg away from one side of the bird, then carve
slices from the breast and from this leg.

To prepare in advance:
If you wish to carve or joint the poultry early do this only
just before the meal, so it does not become dry. Make sure the
serving dish is very hot. Cover carved chicken or turkey with
foil, so the flesh does not become dry.
Put sliced goose or jointed duck with the cut side downwards;
arrange the crisp skin over the meat. Do not cover otherwise
you lose the crispness of the skin.
Serve sage and onion or chestnut stuffing with duck or goose;
parsley and thyme and chestnut stuffing with chicken or
turkey; apple or orange sauce with duck or goose, and
cranberry or bread sauce with chicken or turkey.

Parsley and Thyme Stuffing

Blend together 4 oz. (2 cups) soft breadcrumbs, 1–2
tablespoons chopped parsley, 2 oz. ($\frac{1}{4}$ cup) melted
polyunsaturated margarine, 1–2 teaspoons chopped fresh
thyme or good pinch dried thyme, grated rind and juice of
1 lemon and 1 egg. Season well.

Cranberry Sauce

Make a syrup of $\frac{1}{4}$ pint ($\frac{5}{8}$ cup) water and 2–3 oz. ($\frac{1}{4}$–$\frac{3}{8}$ cup)
sugar. Add 8 oz. cranberries and 2 oz. ($\frac{1}{3}$ cup) sultanas
(golden raisins) and cook until tender. Add 1 tablespoon port
wine if wished. The sauce can be liquidized.

Paprikascsirke
(Hungarian Paprika Chicken)

1 chicken
1 onion
little grated lemon rind
1½ pints (3¾ cups) water
4–5 peppercorns
little salt
bouquet garni

Sauce:
3 oz. (⅜ cup) polyunsaturated
  margarine
4 oz. (1 cup) button mushrooms
1 oz. (¼ cup) flour
1–2 tablespoons paprika
1 pint (2½ cups) stock,
¼ pint (⅔ cup) thick cream (see
  note on Cream, page 12)
seasoning

Joint the chicken – or buy 4 joints of chicken. Chop the
onion. Put the lemon rind, chicken, water and onion into a
pan with the peppercorns, salt and bouquet garni. Simmer
until the chicken is tender. This takes about 45 minutes to
1 hour if young. Lift the chicken from the stock, strain the
stock and keep 1 pint (2½ cups) for the sauce. Either dice the
chicken or keep in the 4 joints.
Heat the margarine in a pan. Toss the mushrooms in the hot
margarine for a few minutes, lift on to a plate. Add the flour
and paprika, stir well for 2–3 minutes over a low heat, then
gradually blend in the stock, bring to the boil and cook,
stirring, until thickened. Put the pieces or joints of chicken
and mushrooms into the sauce. Simmer until thoroughly
heated. Add some of the cream and seasoning, and simmer for
4–5 minutes; do not boil. Top with the remainder of the
cream.
Serves 4–6.

Variations:
Although this particular recipe is more suited to chicken than
other meats you could substitute diced veal or diced very
young lean pork. The cooking time should be slightly longer
for these meats.

To prepare in advance:
If cooking beforehand, take particular care not to over-cook
the chicken.

Chicken Supreme

1 oz. (2 tablespoons)
   polyunsaturated margarine
few finely chopped
   mushrooms or mushroom
   stalks
2 sprigs parsley
1 small onion, finely chopped
1 oz. ($\frac{1}{4}$ cup) flour
$\frac{1}{2}$ pint ($1\frac{1}{4}$ cups) chicken stock
   or water and 1 chicken stock
   cube
2 teaspoons lemon juice

12 oz. cooked chicken, sliced
1 egg yolk
4 tablespoons double (heavy)
   cream (see note on Cream,
   page 12)
salt and pepper
For the rice:
8 oz. (1 cup) long grain refined
   rice
1 pint ($2\frac{1}{2}$ cups) water
1 teaspoon salt
2 tablespoons chopped parsley

Melt margarine in a saucepan. Add the mushrooms, parsley and onion and fry very gently for 5 minutes. Stir in the flour and cook for 1 minute. Gradually stir in the stock or water and stock cube and bring to the boil, stirring all the time. Reduce the heat, cover the pan and simmer very gently for 30 minutes. Strain the sauce and add the lemon juice and sliced chicken. Heat the chicken through for about 5 minutes. Mix the egg yolk with the cream, season and stir in 3 tablespoons hot chicken sauce. Pour the cream mixture into the pan and heat *without boiling*.

Put the rice, water, salt and parsley into a saucepan. Bring to the boil and stir once. Cover and simmer for 15 minutes or until the rice is tender and all the liquid is absorbed. Put the rice round the edge of the serving dish and spoon the chicken and sauce into the centre.

Serves 4.

CHICKEN SUPREME (*Photograph by American Rice Council*)

Desserts, Pies and Flans

With most diets it is the desserts that are the most difficult items to cut out, as anyone with a weakness for sweet things will know. On a low cholesterol diet you can still enjoy your favourite desserts, even with 'cream' (see note on Cream, page 12). Some of the recipes may have an unfamiliar ring to them, as certain ingredients have to be substituted – Shortcrust Pastry (on the opposite page) no longer contains butter but poly-unsaturated margarine; there's no cream in Strawberry Cream Pie (page 63), but instant dessert topping makes a very good second best; and custard served as an accompaniment should be made with low fat milk powder. Simple changes, these make little or no difference to the flavour.
There are very few desserts that cannot be made to fit into a low cholesterol diet, as the tempting selection that follows shows only too well.

Shortcrust Pastry

8 oz. (2 cups) flour, preferably
   plain
pinch salt

4 oz. ($\frac{1}{2}$ cup) polyunsaturated
   margarine
cold water to mix

Sieve the flour and salt. Cut the fat into convenient-sized pieces and drop into the bowl. Rub in with the tips of your fingers until the mixture looks like fine breadcrumbs. Do not overhandle. Lift the flour and fat as you rub them together so you incorporate as much air as possible and keep the mixture cool. Gradually add water to give enough moisture to bind the ingredients together. Use a palette knife to blend. Flour varies a great deal in the amount of liquid it absorbs, but you should require about 2 tablespoons water. When blended, form into a neat ball of dough with your fingers. Put on to a lightly floured pastry board, and roll out to a neat oblong or round about $\frac{1}{4}$ inch in thickness unless the recipe states to the contrary. Always roll in one direction and do not turn the rolling pin, instead lift and turn the pastry. This makes sure it is not stretched badly.

Cook as the individual recipes. Generally shortcrust pastry needs a hot oven, 425–450°F, Mark 7–8, to set the pastry, but you may need to reduce the heat after a time.

Variations:
Sweet shortcrust pastry: Add up to 2 tablespoons sugar to the flour and salt.
Nut pastry: Add up to 2 tablespoons finely chopped nuts to the flour, etc. This is delicious with fruit pies.

To prepare in advance:
Store the uncooked pastry in wrapped foil or polythene (plastic) in the refrigerator or freezer or bake the pastry shell and store in an airtight tin.

Fruit Queen of Puddings

2 tablespoons jam
2 oz. (1 cup) soft breadcrumbs
2 eggs
¾ pint (2 cups) milk (see note on Milk, page 11)

3 oz. (⅜ cup) castor (superfine) sugar
3 tablespoons diced fresh or canned fruit

Spread half the jam in an oven-proof dish. Add the crumbs. Separate the egg yolks and make the custard using the yolks, milk and 2 tablespoons sugar. Pour over the crumbs and bake at 300°F, Mark 2, for 45 minutes, until firm. Spread with the jam and most of the fruit. Whip egg whites until very stiff, fold in remaining sugar. Pile on to the custard and top with the remaining fruit. Bake for 15 minutes in a moderate oven, 350°F, Mark 4. Serve hot.
Serves 4.

Lemon Cheese Tart

shortcrust pastry made with 6 oz. (1½ cups) flour, etc. (see previous page)
1 lemon

8 oz. (1 cup) cottage cheese, sieved
2 eggs
2 oz. (¼ cup) sugar

Roll out the pastry and line an 8-inch pie plate. Bake blind as the flan on page 63, in a hot oven for 15 minutes only. Mix the grated rind and juice of the lemon with the cottage cheese, beaten eggs and sugar. Spoon into the pastry case, return to the oven, lowering the temperature to moderate, 350°F, Mark 4, and continue baking for a further 25 minutes until firm and golden. Serve cold.
Serves 4–6.

Flaky Pastry

8 oz. (2 cups) flour, preferably
   plain
pinch salt

6 oz. (¾ cup) polyunsaturated
   margarine
water to mix, as cold as possible

Sieve the flour and salt into a mixing bowl. Rub in one third of the fat. Add enough water to make an elastic dough. Roll out to an oblong on a lightly floured board. Divide the remaining fat in half, if hard soften by pressing with a knife. Put over the top two-thirds of the pastry in small pieces. Bring up the bottom third of the pastry dough and fold like an envelope. Bring down the top third.

Turn the pastry at right angles, seal the ends of the pastry then depress this at regular intervals with a lightly floured rolling pin. This is called 'ribbing' the pastry. Roll the dough out into an oblong shape again. If you find it feels sticky and is difficult to roll then put away in a cool place for another 30 minutes, or longer if wished. Repeat the process described above, using rest of the fat. Roll out to the required shape, chill until ready to use.

Cook as the individual recipe, but flaky pastry needs a hot to very hot oven to encourage the pastry to rise and to prevent it being greasy. Serve hot or cold.

Variation:
Rough Puff Pastry: Use the same proportions of fat as for Flaky Pastry, but put this into the flour and salt. Cut into tiny pieces and blend with water, or water and a squeeze of lemon juice. Roll out to an oblong shape, fold as for flaky pastry and continue the method of rolling. Allow 5 rollings and 5 foldings in all.

Strawberry Cream Pie

sweet shortcrust pastry (see
  page 59)
$1\frac{1}{2}$ lb. (scant 5 cups) firm
  strawberries
generous $\frac{1}{4}$ pint (good $\frac{2}{3}$ cup)
thick cream (see note on
Cream, page 12)

2–4 oz. ($\frac{1}{4}$–$\frac{1}{2}$ cup) sugar
$\frac{1}{4}$ pint ($\frac{2}{3}$ cup) water
$1\frac{1}{2}$ level teaspoons arrowroot or
  cornflour (cornstarch)

Roll out the pastry and line an 8-inch flan ring, which has
been set on an up-turned baking tin, or a flan dish. Fill with
greaseproof (waxed) paper, crusts of bread or beans, or with
foil. Bake empty, this is called baking 'blind', for about
15 minutes until set, in the centre of a moderately hot oven,
375–400°F, Mark 5–6, then remove paper, bread, beans or
foil. Continue baking the flan case until golden brown, then
cool.
Slice about half the strawberries neatly and mash the rest. Mix
the mashed strawberries with most of the whipped cream and
some of the sugar and put into the pastry case. Blend the rest
of the sugar – the amount depends upon personal taste, the
water and arrowroot or cornflour (cornstarch) in a saucepan.
Stir over a low heat until thick and clear. Add the sliced
strawberries, heat for 1 minute only, then allow mixture to
become cold. Spoon over the cream mixture and decorate with
the last of the cream.
Serves 5–6.

Fritter Batter

4 oz. (1 cup) plain (all-purpose) flour
pinch salt
2 eggs

$\frac{1}{4}$ pint ($\frac{2}{3}$ cup) milk (see note on Milk, page 11)
1–2 teaspoons oil

Sieve the flour and salt. Gradually beat in the eggs and liquid to form a smooth batter. Add oil just before cooking. For a lighter texture separate the eggs. Add the yolks to the flour, then the milk and oil. Fold the stiffly beaten egg whites into the mixture just before coating the fruit. Economical batter: Use one egg only.

Apple Fritters

fritter batter (above)
1 tablespoon flour
oil for deep frying

4 good-sized cooking apples
sugar to coat

Prepare the batter as the recipe in a large basin (this makes it easier to coat the fruit). Put the flour on a large plate. Heat the oil. To test if it is at the correct temperature, drop a cube of bread into it. The bread should turn golden in 30 seconds. Lower the heat so the oil does not over-heat. Peel and core the apples, then cut into $\frac{1}{2}$-inch rings.

Coat the fruit first with flour (this makes sure the batter adheres well) and then with the batter. Lift out with a fork, hold over the basin and allow surplus to drop into the basin.

Drop into the hot oil and cook steadily for 4–5 minutes until golden brown. Lift out, drain on absorbent paper, coat in sugar and serve hot.

Serves 4.

Beignets Aux Cerises
(French Cherry Fritters)

Sauce:
1 lb. black or Morello cherries
$\frac{1}{4}$ pint ($\frac{2}{3}$ cup) water
2–4 oz. ($\frac{1}{4}$–$\frac{1}{2}$ cup) sugar
1 teaspoon arrowroot
3–4 tablespoons cherry brandy

Choux pastry:
$\frac{1}{4}$ pint ($\frac{2}{3}$ cup) water
1 oz. (2 tablespoons)
   polyunsaturated margarine
3 oz. ($\frac{3}{4}$ cup) plain (all-purpose)
   flour
pinch sugar
2 eggs
1 egg yolk
oil for frying

Put the cherries, water and sugar into a pan and simmer for about 5 minutes. Blend the arrowroot with the cherry brandy, stir into the cherry mixture, boil steadily, stirring well, until thickened. Keep hot.

Heat the water and margarine in a saucepan. When margarine has melted add the flour, sieved with sugar. Stir the mixture over a low heat until it forms a firm ball. Remove the pan from the heat and gradually add the beaten eggs and egg yolk.

Heat the oil to about 365°F, i.e. until a cube of day-old bread turns golden brown in about 30 seconds. Either put spoonfuls of the mixture into the hot oil, or put the choux pastry into a cloth bag with a 1-inch plain pipe. Squeeze the choux pastry through the pipe with one hand and cut off $1-1\frac{1}{2}$-inch lengths with kitchen scissors. Fry steadily for about 6–8 minutes until golden brown, lift out of the oil, drain on absorbent paper. Keep hot on a flat dish in a low oven.

Pile fritters into a pyramid and serve with the hot sauce.

Serves 6–8.

To complete the meal:
As this dessert is rich and satisfying and also demands a considerable amount of attention when cooking, precede with a salad.

To serve for a buffet:
Only suitable if you have quite an elaborate table cooker.

Crêpes Suzette

French citrus crêpes

6 oz. (1½ cups) flour
pinch salt
2 eggs
¾ pint (2 cups) milk (see note on
   Milk, page 11)
oil for frying
Filling:
2–3 oz. (¼–⅜ cup)
   polyunsaturated margarine
finely grated rind 2 oranges or
   4 tangerines

3 oz. (nearly ¾ cup) icing
   (confectioners') sugar
little orange or tangerine juice
Sauce:
2 oz. (¼ cup) castor (superfine)
   sugar
juice of 2 oranges or 4 tangerines
juice of 1 small lemon
2–3 tablespoons Curaçao or
   Cointreau

Make the crêpe batter by beating the flour, salt, eggs and milk together. Fry spoonfuls of the batter in a very little hot oil to give about 12 thin crêpes. Blend all the ingredients for the filling together, add just enough fruit juice to give the consistency of thick cream. Put some of the filling into the centre of each cooked crêpe, then fold in four.

Put the sugar into a large pan and heat over a low heat until it just begins to turn golden brown. Add the fruit juice and blend with the sugar. Heat the crêpes very gently in the hot sauce. Add the Curaçao or Cointreau just before serving. Ignite if wished.

Serves 6.

Variations:

Although oranges or tangerines are the accepted filling, orange marmalade or red currant jelly could be put into the crêpes. Thin shreds of peel can be soaked, then heated in the sauce with the crêpes.

Although not really part of the classic dish, you can decorate with slices of orange.

Baking

Home baking is a very satisfying occupation, and it works out cheaper to make your own breads, cakes and biscuits (cookies), especially if you 'batch bake'. When the oven is on, make the most of the heat, rather than baking just one cake. Many items require the same temperature, and it makes sense to fill each shelf.

As with desserts, most breads, cakes and biscuits (cookies) are allowed – there is just the odd recipe amendment here and there. You'll never know the difference.

All the old favourites are included in this chapter, such as White and Wholemeal Bread (pages 70–72), Vanilla Slices (page 74) and Shortbread Biscuits (page 75), as well as some new treats – Orange Cheese Cake (page 76) and Mocha Hazel-nut Gâteau (page 80).

Basic White Bread

*As the process is lengthy, and cooked bread freezes excellently, I have given
the recipe based on 3 lb. (12 cups) flour to make several small loaves. If
you want to make just one loaf then use 1 lb. (4 cups) flour and reduce all
ingredients in proportion, except the yeast. Use ½ oz. fresh yeast or dried
yeast in proportion. If you can buy strong flour, you have a better result.
Failing this use plain flour.*

3 lb. (12 cups) strong flour	1 teaspoon sugar
3 teaspoons salt	approximately 1½ pints (3¾ cups)
1 oz. yeast	tepid water

Sieve the flour and salt into a warm bowl. Cream the yeast
with the sugar, add most of the liquid. Make a well in the
centre of the bowl of flour, pour in the yeast liquid and
sprinkle flour on top. Cover the bowl with a clean cloth and
leave for about 20 minutes, until the surface is covered with
bubbles. Mix the liquid with the flour, if too dry then add
sufficient tepid liquid to give an elastic dough. Turn out of the
bowl on to a floured board and knead until smooth. Either
put back into the bowl and cover with a cloth or put into a
large greased polythene bag. Leave to rise until almost double
the original size. Turn on to the board again and knead. Form
into the shaped loaves you like; for a tin loaf grease, flour and
warm the tins. Form the dough into an oblong shape, fold into
three to fit the tin and lower into the tin. The dough should
come just over half-way up the tins. If you brush the loaves
with a little oil it produces an excellent crust. Cover the tins
with a cloth or polythene (plastic) and leave the loaves to rise
for 20 minutes.

Bake for about 20–25 minutes in the centre of a hot oven,
425°F, Mark 7; after this lower the heat to moderate, 350°F,
Mark 4, and complete cooking. A 1-lb. (4-cup) tin loaf takes
a total of about 35–40 minutes.

To test the bread turn the loaves out of the tins, knock firmly
on the base. The bread should sound hollow. If it does not,
return to the oven for a little longer.

Makes 3 loaves.

Variations:

Using fat: Rub 2–3 oz. ($\frac{1}{4}$–$\frac{3}{8}$ cup) polyunsaturated margarine into the flour.

Milk loaf: Blend with milk instead of water (see note on Milk, page 11).

Fruit loaf: Add 6 oz. (1 cup) dried fruit and 2–4 oz. ($\frac{1}{4}$–$\frac{1}{2}$ cup) sugar to the flour. Bake the loaves as the basic recipe. When they come from the oven top with a sugar and water glaze.

To glaze 3 loaves: Blend 2–3 oz. ($\frac{1}{4}$–$\frac{3}{8}$ cup) sugar with 2 tablespoons boiling water. Brush over the bread. The same glaze can be used for topping buns.

Hamburger Rolls: The recipe for bread can be adapted to make the soft hamburger rolls. Be a little more generous with the amount of liquid in the recipe, adding this until you produce a very slightly sticky dough. Knead, as given in the recipe. Allow to rise. Knead again and form into rounds. Put the rolls on to the warmed baking trays, allowing plenty of room for them to spread out, then flatten the rounds slightly with your hands. Allow to rise as for bread, but this takes only approximately 15 minutes with rolls. Bake for 12 minutes towards the top of a very hot oven, 450–500°F, Mark 8–10. 1 lb. (4 cups) flour etc., makes 12–14 large rolls.

Crisp Topped Rolls: Recipe as for bread, but be a little more sparing with the liquid and these are better mixed with milk rather than water, and with a small amount of margarine rubbed into the flour. Allow the dough to rise, as for bread, then form into small rounds, batons or other shapes. Brush with beaten egg then a little melted margarine and allow to rise for approximately 15 minutes, then bake for about 12 minutes towards the top of a very hot oven, 450–500°F, Mark 8–10. 1 lb. (4 cups) flour etc., makes about 18–20 small rolls.

Baking Powder Rolls: Sieve 8 oz. (2 cups) self-raising flour or plain (all-purpose) flour with 2 teaspoons baking powder and a pinch salt. Bind with milk or milk and water to make a slightly sticky dough. Knead lightly for 1 minute on a floured board. Divide into 8 portions, put on an ungreased baking tray and cook as for previous recipe.

Plain Buns

½ oz. yeast
2 oz. (¼ cup) sugar
just under ½ pint (1¼ cups) tepid
   water or milk (see note on
   Milk, page 11)

1 lb. (4 cups) plain (all-purpose)
   flour
good pinch salt
1 oz. (2 tablespoons)
   polyunsaturated margarine
1 egg

This is a good starting point for yeast cookery as imperfections of handling are less noticeable than when making bread. You can add fruit to the basic ingredients above or top the cooked buns with some kind of icing or use this for doughnuts. The process of making is as Basic White Bread (see page 70).

Wholemeal Bread

1 tablespoon sugar
1 tablespoon active dried yeast
1 tablespoon vegetable fat

½ teaspoon salt
1 lb. (4 cups) medium or coarse
   stoneground wholemeal flour

This is a very firm textured bread. Use fine wholemeal flour for a lighter texture, or half of wholemeal flour, quarter of millet flour and quarter of plain (all-purpose) flour.
Dissolve ½ teaspoon sugar in ⅕ pint (½ cup) hand-hot water. Sprinkle the yeast into this and whisk with a fork. Stand it in a warm place for 10–15 minutes.
Dissolve the remaining sugar in ⅖ pint (1 cup) warm water, together with the fat and salt. Add to the flour along with the yeast mixture and mix until a smooth dough is formed. Leave to stand in a warm place for approximately 30 minutes.
Knead lightly and shape into a loaf. Put into an oiled loaf tin and leave to rise in a warm place for 30 minutes.
Bake in a hot oven, 425°F, Mark 7, for 35–40 minutes until cooked. When cooked, the loaf should sound hollow when knocked with the knuckles.
Makes 1 loaf.

Vanilla Slices (Milles Feuilles)

puff pastry made with 8 oz.
  (2 cups) flour, etc.
Filling:
½ pint (1¼ cups) thick cream (see
  note on Cream, page 12)
sugar to taste

few drops vanilla essence
jam or jelly
little sifted icing (confectioners')
  sugar

Roll the pastry out until wafer thin. Cut into about 15 or 18 fingers. Put on to baking trays or sheets, leave in a cool place for about 30 minutes; this makes sure they keep a good shape.
Bake just above the centre of a very hot oven, 450°F, Mark 8. Bake for approximately 10 minutes at this high temperature until well risen and golden, then lower the heat to moderate, 350°F, Mark 4, or switch the oven off for about 5 minutes. Allow to cool then trim the edges with a very sharp knife. Whip the cream, add a little sugar and vanilla essence. Spread one-third of the slices with the cream, top with another slice, then with the jam or jelly and a final pastry slice. Dust with icing (confectioners') sugar.

Makes 5 or 6.

Note: Flaky or rough puff are not as good in this recipe as puff pastry.

Variations:
Three layers of pastry give a tall and very impressive slice, but two layers of pastry are often used, in which case spread the bottom layer of pastry with jam or jelly and then with cream, and top with the second layer of pastry.
Coat the top of the slices with glacé icing.

Economy hint:
Fill the slices with vanilla cream (page 94) instead of whipped cream.

To prepare in advance:
Make and bake the pastry and store in an airtight tin away from cakes. Reheat gently if the pastry has lost its crispness, cool then fill.

Strawberry Shortcake

8 oz. (2 cups) self-raising flour
2 oz. ($\frac{1}{4}$ cup) polyunsaturated
   margarine
2 oz. ($\frac{1}{4}$ cup) sugar
milk to mix

Filling:
little sugar
strawberries
thick cream (see notes on Milk
   and Cream, pages 11–12)

Sieve the flour into a mixing bowl and rub in the margarine. Add the sugar and mix to a fairly firm rolling consistency with the milk. Knead the dough lightly to give a smooth mixture. Divide into two equal portions and form into two 8–9-inch rounds. Put into lightly oiled 8–9-inch sandwich or shallow cake tins. Bake just above the centre of a hot oven, 425–450°F, Mark 6–7, for about 15 minutes or until firm and golden brown. Turn out, allow to cool, then sandwich together with sweetened fruit and whipped cream. Top with fruit and cream.
Serves 4–6.
This is the most economical type of shortcake that can be varied in very many ways.

Shortbread Biscuits (Cookies)

4 oz. ($\frac{1}{2}$ cup) polyunsaturated
   margarine
3 oz. ($\frac{3}{4}$ cup) sieved icing
   (confectioners') sugar

6 oz. ($1\frac{1}{2}$ cups) plain (all-purpose)
   flour
flavouring

Cream the margarine and sugar until soft. Add the flour and flavouring, and knead well until smooth. Roll out to about $\frac{1}{4}$ inch in thickness. Cut into fingers or rounds. Put on to an ungreased baking tray and prick with a fork, this prevents the mixture rising, and bake in the centre of a very moderate oven, 325°F, Mark 3. Cool on the baking tray.
Flavourings:
Add the grated rind, but not juice, of a lemon.
Add a good pinch mixed spice or other spice.
Variation:
Shortbread Round: Use recipe above or increase fat by 1 oz. (2 tablespoons). Press into an 8-inch tin. Prick, and bake for 30 minutes in very moderate oven, 325°F, Mark 3.

Orange Cheese Cake

Coating:

6 oz. digestive biscuits (graham crackers)

2 oz. (¼ cup) polyunsaturated margarine

1 tablespoon honey

grated rind 2 oranges

2 oz. (¼ cup) castor (superfine) sugar

Filling:

2 oz. (¼ cup) polyunsaturated margarine

grated rind 1 orange

3 oz. (⅜ cup) castor (superfine) sugar

2 eggs, separated

1 oz. (¼ cup) cornflour (cornstarch)

12 oz. (1½ cups) cottage cheese

2 tablespoons orange juice

To decorate:

little sieved icing (confectioners') sugar

canned mandarin oranges

Crush the biscuits (crackers) until most of them are very fine, but keep some crumbs a little coarser (see the picture). Cream margarine, honey, orange rind and sugar. Add the crumbs and use to line the sides and bottom of a 7–8-inch cake tin – choose a tin with a loose base.

Cream margarine, orange rind and castor (superfine) sugar. Add the egg yolks, cornflour (cornstarch), cottage cheese (sieved if wished, but it is not essential) and orange juice. Lastly fold in the stiffly whisked egg whites. Spoon into the biscuit case and bake for approximately 1¼ hours in the centre of a slow to very moderate oven, 300–325°F, Mark 2–3, until firm but pale golden. Allow to cool in the oven with the heat turned off (this stops the cake sinking).

Remove from the tin. Sprinkle icing (confectioners') sugar over the cheese cake and decorate with well drained mandarin orange segments.

Serves 7–8.

Gold Ginger Loaf

10 oz. (2½ cups) plain (all-purpose) flour
1 teaspoon bicarbonate of soda (baking soda)
½ teaspoon ground ginger
6 oz. (¾ cup) clear honey
4 oz. (½ cup) polyunsaturated margarine
6 oz. (¾ cup) sugar
2 tablespoons syrup from jar of preserved ginger
1½ tablespoons milk (see note on Milk, page 11)
2 eggs
Decoration:
1 tablespoon honey
few leaves angelica
2–3 tablespoons preserved ginger, cut in neat pieces

Sieve the dry ingredients into the mixing bowl.
To weigh the honey: Put an empty saucepan on the scales, note the weight, then add 6 oz. (½ cup) honey, or syrup – see variation.
To measure the honey: If the measuring cup is floured the honey, or syrup – see variation – pours out easily into the saucepan. Add the fat and sugar to honey in the pan. Heat gently until the fat melts, pour over the flour and beat well. Warm the ginger syrup and milk in the pan, add to the flour mixture with the eggs and beat until smooth. Line a 2½–3 lb. loaf tin with greased greaseproof (waxed) paper. Pour in the mixture. Bake in the centre of a slow to very moderate oven, 300–325°F, Mark 2–3, for 1–1¼ hours until just firm to the touch, do not over-cook. Remove from the oven, cool in the tin for about 15 minutes. Remove from the tin, take off the paper, then brush the top with the honey and press the pieces of angelica and ginger into position.
Serve as a cake with coffee or tea, or spread with polyunsaturated margarine as a tea-bread. This is also delicious sliced and topped with apple purée.

Variation:
To make a darker loaf, use either golden (light corn) syrup or black treacle or a mixture of these, in place of the honey. The amount of ground ginger may be increased to 2 teaspoons, as the above recipe has a very mild flavour.

Scotch Pancakes

4 oz. (1 cup) flour*
pinch salt
1 egg

$\frac{1}{4}$ pint ($\frac{2}{3}$ cup) milk (see note on
  Milk, page 11)
little oil

*Use either self-raising flour, or plain (all-purpose) flour with 1 level teaspoon baking powder, or plain (all-purpose) flour with $\frac{1}{4}$ teaspoon bicarbonate of soda (baking soda) and $\frac{1}{2}$ teaspoon cream of tartar

Sieve the self-raising flour, or flour and raising agent, well with the salt. Add the egg and beat, then gradually whisk in the milk or milk and water to give a smooth batter.

The old-fashioned griddle, sometimes called a girdle or bakestone, has become difficult to find, but modern versions are being made. The alternatives are to use a solid hotplate on an electric cooker, again becoming less plentiful with modern-type cookers, or a frying pan. If the frying pan is heavy then use it in the normal way, but if it is light-weight the scones are inclined to burn and I find the best thing is to turn the frying pan upside-down and cook the scones on the base.

Grease the griddle with oil and heat. Test by dropping a teaspoon of the batter mixture on to the warm plate; the batter should set almost at once and begin to bubble within 1 minute. If this does not happen then heat the griddle a little longer before cooking the scones.

Drop the scone mixture from a tablespoon on to the griddle and cook for 1–2 minutes until the top surface is covered with bubbles. Put a palette knife under the scone and turn carefully; cook for the same time on the second side. To test if cooked, press gently with the edge of the knife and if no batter oozes out then the scones are cooked. Lift on to a clean teacloth on a wire cooling tray and wrap in the cloth until ready to serve.

Serve cold or warm topped with polyunsaturated margarine and jam; or with cooked, well drained fruit, as a quick and easy dessert. These are also excellent served with baked beans as a supper snack.

Makes 10–12.

Mocha Hazel-Nut Gâteau

6 oz. ($\frac{3}{4}$ cup) polyunsaturated
   margarine
6 oz. ($\frac{3}{4}$ cup) castor (superfine)
   sugar
3 large eggs
5 oz. ($1\frac{1}{4}$ cups) self-raising flour,
   or use plain (all-purpose) flour
   with $1\frac{1}{4}$ teaspoons baking
   powder (baking soda)
2 tablespoons cocoa
$1\frac{1}{2}$ oz. ($\frac{1}{4}$ cup) very finely
   chopped hazel-nuts
1 tablespoon strong coffee

Filling:
10–12 oz. ($1\frac{1}{4}$–$1\frac{1}{2}$ cups)
   polyunsaturated margarine
1–$1\frac{1}{4}$ lb. (3–$3\frac{3}{4}$ cups) sieved
   icing (confectioners') sugar
1–$1\frac{1}{2}$ tablespoons strong coffee
3–4 tablespoons chopped
   hazel-nuts
whole hazel-nuts to decorate

Cream the margarine and sugar together, and gradually add the beaten eggs. Then fold in the self-raising flour or plain (all-purpose) flour and baking powder and cocoa. Add the chopped hazel-nuts and coffee. Divide the mixture between two 8–$8\frac{1}{2}$-inch greased and floured sandwich tins and bake for 20–25 minutes above the centre of a moderate oven, 350–375°F, Mark 4–5 until firm to the touch. Turn out carefully and allow to cool.

Make coffee filling and icing by creaming the margarine with the icing (confectioners') sugar and coffee; the variation in amounts depends on the thickness and firmness preferred. Use about $\frac{1}{4}$ of the mixture to sandwich the cakes together and another $\frac{1}{4}$ to coat the sides. Roll the cake in the chopped nuts, then cover the top of the cake with some of the remaining icing. Pipe rosettes on top with the last of the icing. Decorate with whole hazel-nuts.

Gives 8–10 slices.

To prepare in advance:
Although the cake keeps reasonably well for several days it will keep even better if it is iced, then stored in an airtight tin, or frozen and wrapped in polythene (plastic).

Economy hint:
Hazel-nuts are expensive so use chopped walnuts instead in both the cake and the icing.

Drinks, Sauces and Extras

Here you will find a drink to suit every taste – Fresh Lemon Drink and Garden Cocktail (page 86) for teetotallers, and Wine Cup (page 84) for those who like something with a bit more punch.

The basic White Sauce (page 88) with suggested variations, and the Béarnaise Sauce (page 90) will turn a simple dish into something rather special, without a great deal of effort.

In a miscellany of recipes, one expects to find at least one trespasser; a dish that is quite different, with no others like it. Breakfast Muesli and Apple Muesli with Yoghurt (page 91) are tasty alternatives to the more traditional breakfast cereal, and Garlic Bread (page 90) adds extra meal appeal to any soup, hot or cold.

Choosing Wines

Never let price be your only consideration when buying wines. There are some excellent inexpensive wines.

It is wise to sample an unfamiliar wine before offering it at a party; buy $\frac{1}{2}$ a bottle beforehand and try it out. Individual bottles may vary slightly, but this should give you a good idea of the quality of the particular wine. When buying the large amount check it is the same year as the sample you tried. Allow about $\frac{1}{2}$ bottle of wine per person.

Serve white wines and rosé wines well chilled. Do not over-chill though, otherwise they lose their flavour.

Serve red wines at room temperature, and try and draw the corks about an hour before serving if possible.

The suggestion of serving a white wine with fish, poultry and mild flavoured dishes is simply that the flavour is more delicate and blends better with these kinds of food, just as the more full-flavoured and robust red wines blend with beef, game and dishes that are strong in taste. A rosé wine is a good 'mixer' with most foods.

The following are just some of the most familiar wines.

Red Wines:
Nuits St. George; Beaune; Beaujolais; Pommard; Mouton-Rothchild; Médoc St. Emilion; Volnay; Valpolicello (Italian).

White Wines:
Pouilly-Fuissé; Graves; Meursault; Puligny-Montrachet; Riesling (German); Soave di Verona (Italian).

Rosé Wines:
Tavel rosé; Graves rosé; Mateus rosé (Portuguese).

Wine Drinks

The following wine cup is an example of the way in which inexpensive wine can be used to make an interesting drink. It is ideal for buffet parties.
Cider, alcoholic or non-alcoholic for children, could be used in place of the white wine; omit the brandy and add ginger ale for additional flavour.

Wine Cup

2 lemons
1–2 oranges
$\frac{1}{2}$ pint (1$\frac{1}{4}$ cups) water
2–3 oz. ($\frac{1}{4}$–$\frac{3}{8}$ cup) sugar
ice cubes
2 bottles white wine

miniature bottle or wineglass
 brandy
Decoration:
cucumber slices
orange slices
sprigs borage or mint, optional

Pare the rind from the lemons and oranges very thinly. Squeeze out the juice and put on one side. Simmer the peel in the water for about 5 minutes. Add the sugar and stir until dissolved. Strain and allow to cool, then blend with the fruit juices.
Put the ice into a serving bowl, add the fruit mixture, wine and brandy. Stir gently to mix, then decorate with the cucumber, orange slices and herbs, when these are available. All recipes based on this make about 16 glasses, unless stated otherwise.

Variations:
Use only $\frac{1}{4}$ pint ($\frac{2}{3}$ cup) water with the fruit rinds.
Use weak, well strained China tea in place of water.
Use a rosé wine and Maraschino instead of white wine and brandy, top with sliced peaches and cherries.
Use only $\frac{1}{4}$ pint ($\frac{2}{3}$ cup) water, then add $\frac{1}{2}$ pint (1$\frac{1}{4}$ cups) soda water just before serving.

Fresh Lemon Drink

3 large lemons
4 oz. ($\frac{1}{2}$ cup) sugar
2 pints (5 cups) boiling water

3 sprigs mint
2 cups cracked ice
4 slices lemon

Wash whole lemons, then cut into $\frac{1}{2}$-inch cubes, taking care
not to lose the juice.
Put into a large stoneware jug, add the sugar, and pour on
boiling water. Leave approximately 20 minutes, then strain.
Add mint, ice and slices of fresh lemon to lemon drink.
Allow ice to cool drink, then serve.
Serves 6–8.

Garden Cocktail

2 large apples
$\frac{1}{2}$ lb. carrots
3 sticks celery

ground pepper
crushed walnuts to garnish

Peel apples and carrots, then chop them into $\frac{1}{4}$-inch to
$\frac{1}{2}$-inch cubes. Finely slice celery.
Place chopped fruit and vegetables in liquidizer and blend.
Add pepper to taste.
Pour into glasses and garnish with chopped walnuts.
Serves 3–4.

Note: You will need a powerful liquidizer to mix this
properly. If carrots are very crisp, a juice extractor may be
required. Alternatively, blend ingredients in liquidizer,
substituting canned or home-made carrot juice for whole
carrots.

Iced Lollies

These can be made with ice cream (see note on Cream, page 12). Make up instant dessert topping with 12 fl. oz. (1½ cups) low fat milk and freeze. Alternatively, make more refreshing lollies with fruit juice or fruit purée.
The special moulds in which to freeze lollies are quite inexpensive and should last indefinitely.

Orange Lollies

Squeeze the juice from oranges or rub the pulp through a sieve or emulsify in the liquidizer to give a smooth purée.
To save money the juice or purée can be diluted with a little water or you can simmer the peel with water (for additional flavour) for 5 minutes. Try to avoid using any sugar in sweetening the orange juice or purée – or use the minimum, so that children do not develop a taste for over-sweet foods.
Pour or spoon the juice or purée into the moulds and freeze until very hard – the 'stick' should be placed into position before freezing.
Other fruit juices to use: diluted rose hip syrup, blackcurrant syrup (well diluted), grapefruit, pineapple juice.

Apple Lollies

Simmer apples with a very little water and sugar or honey to taste. The fruit may be flavoured with a little lemon juice. Emulsify or sieve to make a very smooth purée, then freeze in the moulds. Tint a pale green if wished.
These lollies can be made by half filling the moulds with apple purée (coloured with a very few drops of green – do not over-colour), then freezing until firm. Chilled orange juice is then poured into the half filled moulds and the lollies are frozen until both layers are firm.
Other fruit purées to use: sieved fresh raspberries, strawberries, black and red currants, cooked plums.

White Sauce

Coating consistency:
1 oz. (2 tablespoons)
   polyunsaturated margarine
1 oz. (¼ cup) flour

½ pint (1¼ cups) milk (see note on
   Milk, page 11)
seasoning

Heat margarine until it has just melted. Remove pan from the heat, stir in the flour. Return to a low heat and stir for several minutes, until the 'roux' forms a dry looking ball. Once again take the pan off the heat and gradually blend in the liquid. Stir briskly with a wooden spoon as you do so. Return once again to the heat and bring steadily to the boil, stirring or whisking all the time as the sauce thickens. Add a little seasoning and continue stirring for 4–5 minutes, until the sauce coats the back of the spoon, see the picture on the opposite page. Taste and add more seasoning if required.
Serves 3–4.

There are three ways in which the sauce may be made more rapidly:
Blending method: Use the same proportions as above. Blend the flour carefully with the liquid. Put into a saucepan. Add the margarine, and then bring gradually to the boil, stirring all the time. Continue cooking as above.
Quick method: Use the same proportions as above. Prepare the 'roux'. Take the pan off the heat, add all the liquid. Return to the heat. Allow the liquid to come to the boil and whisk sharply. Continue cooking as above.
Using cornflour (cornstarch): You can use cornflour (cornstarch) instead of flour but you need only ½ oz. (2 tablespoons) in place of 1 oz. (¼ cup) flour. Although a sauce made with cornflour (cornstarch) thickens more quickly than one made with flour, it is important to cook it for some minutes.

Variations:
Add a little anchovy essence; chopped parsley or other herbs; 2–4 oz. (⅓–⅔ cup) chopped shrimps; 4 oz. (1 cup) grated cheese (see notes on Cheese and Shellfish, page 11).

Béarnaise Sauce

4 tablespoons white wine vinegar
6 peppercorns
½ bay leaf
1 sprig each of tarragon and
    chervil
2 egg yolks

2½ oz. (5 tablespoons)
    polyunsaturated margarine
salt
1 teaspoon each chopped
    tarragon and chervil

Put the vinegar, peppercorns, bay leaf, tarragon and chervil
sprigs into a small pan. Bring to the boil, then boil until the
quantity is reduced to 1 tablespoon.
Beat the egg yolks with 1 tablespoon of the margarine and a
pinch of salt. Put into a basin over a pan of hot water, or into
a double pan, stir until the mixture begins to thicken then add
the strained vinegar. Mix well and add remaining
margarine a little at a time, stirring continuously with a
wooden spoon until all the margarine is used up and the
sauce thickens. Add the chopped tarragon and chervil and
adjust the seasoning.

Note There are several good quality brands of Béarnaise sauce on the
market if you have no time to make your own.

Garlic Bread

1 long crusty French loaf
2 oz. (¼ cup) polyunsaturated
    margarine

2 garlic cloves
salt, pepper

Cut the bread into even slanting slices, not quite through.
Cream margarine with the crushed garlic and salt and pepper.
Spread each slice of bread generously with the mixture, then
re-shape the loaf.
Wrap in foil and bake for 10 minutes in a hot oven, 425°F,
Mark 7. Reduce the heat to 400°F, Mark 6, open the foil and
return to the oven for about 5 minutes.

Muesli

An instant healthy breakfast food, rich in protein, vitamins and iron. There are many branded mueslis on the market and basically they contain wholegrain cereals, dried fruits, nuts and some skim milk powder and fruit sugars. Most of the ingredients can be bought in bulk at a health food store, which is not only more economical, but means the recipe can be varied to suit the individual taste. Make a basic muesli from wheatmeal, wheatgerm, oat flakes, maize meal and bran and use it as a base for the following dishes.

Breakfast Muesli

4 tablespoons mixed grains
1 tablespoon skim milk powder
1 tablespoon chopped mixed nuts

1 tablespoon raisins
a little dried apple or apricot
sugar to taste

Can be eaten dry with milk, or mixed with water and heated gently until thick and creamy.
Serves 2.

Apple Muesli with Yogurt

6 tablespoons yogurt
2 tablespoons lemon juice
4 tablespoons mixed grains
2 tablespoons honey
6 tablespoons water

1 large apple, peeled, cored and
  grated
2 tablespoons grated hazel nuts
  or almonds

Mix yogurt and lemon juice and add to the grains, stirring well. Add honey, water and apple. Sprinkle nuts over the dish and serve immediately.
Serves 2.

Index

Figures in italics refer to illustrations

The publishers wish to thank the following for their contribution to the book:

John Lee
Norman Nicholls
Syndication International
Bryce Attwell
New Idea magazine
Phoebe's Health Food Shop, Sydney and Mervyn Clark
Casa Pupo Shop, David Jones, Sydney
Crown Corning Pty, Ltd
Incorporated Agencies Pty, Ltd, Sydney
Opus Design Shop, Sydney
Phil Dunn by courtesy of The Potters Gallery, Sydney
Rosenthall Studio-Line, Sydney
The Bay Tree Pty. Ltd, Sydney
Vasa Agencies Pty. Ltd, Sydney